An Album
of American
Women

AN ALBUM OF AMERICAN WOMEN

THEIR CHANGING ROLE

GLORIA D. INGRAHAM
LEONARD W. INGRAHAM

FRANKLIN WATTS

NEW YORK • LONDON • TORONTO • SYDNEY • 1987

Photographs courtesy of: Schlesinger Library, Radcliffe College: pp. 6 (top), 11 (top), 15 (top), 16 (top right, middle left, and bottom), 20, 22, 24 (top and bottom), 35 (top), 41; New York Public Library Picture Collection: pp. 6 (bottom left), 13 (middle right and bottom right), 15 (bottom), 23, 28 (top), 49 (bottom), 51 (both); Bettye Lane: pp. 6 (bottom right), 35 (bottom right and left), 56 (bottom), 62 (top right), 67 (top left and bottom), 69 (middle), 76 (all), 77 (top and bottom); The Bettmann Archive, Inc.: pp. 8, 11 (bottom), 12, 13 (top left), 30, 31; Sophia Smith Collection: pp. 13 (bottom left), 24 (middle), 25 (all), 46 (top), 49 (top), 77 (middle); The New-York Historical Society: p. 17; The Kansas State Historical Society, Topeka: pp. 19, 43 (top); Monkmeyer: pp. 27 (Rhoda Sidney), 29 (Paul Conklin), 73 (Michael Kagan), 79 (top left-Hugh Rogers); General Electric: p. 28 (bottom); UPI/Bettmann Newsphotos: pp. 37 (top), 38 (bottom right), 55, 58, 61 (top right), 64 (bottom), 66, 68, 69 (top and bottom), 70, 83 (bottom left), 85; National Education Association/Joe Di Dio: pp. 37 (bottom), 43 (bottom), 84 (top left); Meris Powell: p. 38 (top left); National Women's Political Caucus: p. 38 (bottom left); NASA: p. 44 (top and middle); Bob Harper: p. 44 (bottom); Oberlin College: pp. 46 (bottom-John Seyfried); Collections of The Archives of Labor and Urban Affairs, University Archives, Wayne State University: pp. 52, 53 (bottom); National Archives: p. 53 (top); First Women's Bank: p. 56 (top); The Pace Gallery: p. 61 (top left); Frohring Art Center, Hiram College, Hiram, Ohio: p. 61 (bottom); Doubleday & Company, Inc.: p. 62 (bottom left) Jerry Pauer; AP/Wide World Photos: p. 62 (bottom right); Lockheed: p. 64 (top); American Museum of Natural History: p. 64 (middle); Cold Spring Harbor Laboratory, Research Library Archives: p. 65 (top-David Micklos); The New York Times: p. 65 (middle-Bob Glass); Official U.S. Navy Photo: p. 65 (bottom-James S. Davis); Christian Steiner: p. 67 (top right); WNET/Thirteen: p. 71; Tere LoPrete: p. 79 (top right); AFL-CIO: pp. 79 (bottom), 92 (bottom); Lawrence Frank: p. 83 (top); The New York Hospital/Cornell Medical Center: pp. 83 (bottom right), 88; U.S. Air Force Photo: p. 84 (top right); AT&T Corporate Archive: p. 84 (bottom); Michigan Historical Collections, Bentley Historical Library, University of Michigan: p. 89 (Richard Lee); Photo Researchers, Inc.: p. 90 (top-Guy Gillette), (bottom-David M. Grossman); Smith College, School of Social Work: p. 92 (top).

Cover photographs courtesy of: NASA (top left); New York Public Library Picture Collection (top middle); Bettye Lane (top right and bottom left); Schlesinger Library, Radcliffe College (bottom right).

Library of Congress Cataloging-in-Publication Data

Ingraham, Gloria D.
An album of American women.

Bibliography: p.
Includes index.
Summary: A history of the American woman's struggle
for equal rights, with brief biographies of women
distinguished in a number of fields of endeavor.
1. Women's rights—United States—Juvenile
literature.   2. Women social reformers—United
States—Juvenile literature.   3. Women—United
States—History—Juvenile literature.   [1. Women's
rights.   2. Biography]   I. Ingraham, Leonard W.
II. Title.
HQ1236.5.U6I54 1987   305.4′2′0973   87-10466
ISBN 0-531-10317-X

C O N T E N T S

INTRODUCTION

Women's struggle for equal rights is not just part of the recent past. It is a thread that runs through the entire fabric of U.S. history. From the early settlement at Plymouth on the New England coast, throughout our nation's development—its industrial growth, its political changes, its wars, its labor movements—women have fought for their rights and for the rights of others.

The road to equality has been arduous. Women have had to organize, have had to fight their way through state legislatures and congressional obstacles, have had to face ridicule and indifference. Without the means of money and political power, they have often found their way blocked, and only through true grit and determination have they made impressive achievements.

There is still a long road ahead, with many obstacles to overcome. And history shows us that rights dearly gained are easily lost if we fail to consider them precious and to safeguard them.

The chapters that follow will spell out the ways successes have been achieved and the obstacles to equality. You will learn within these pages what life was like for most American women, and you will meet those women who pioneered in fields and professions that previously had been closed to them. The resistance they met became challenges. Their persistence and courage helped pull down the walls.

This book cannot tell you about all of the women—many of them aren't even known—but we will try to show you some who led the way. That equality can be achieved is no longer in doubt. You, the reader and future citizen, will play a part in this struggle; you will help determine whether someday there will indeed be a "gender-free" world.

*The colonial household produced most
of the products it needed. Here women
are making their own candles.*

C H A P T E R 1

HISTORIC BARRIERS TO WOMEN

The Plymouth colony, established in 1620, was one of families, who brought with them the traditions of their English backgrounds. In this early colonial society, women had no standing in the eyes of the law. They did not have the right to own or inherit property. They could not vote or hold any office in government. Married women, under English common law, could not sign contracts, have their own money, or sue for divorce. Basically, women had no political or legal rights and were without political representation. Women often could not speak out; their husbands spoke for them.

In addition to bearing and caring for the children (an average of nine in the colonial household), women worked long hours in the fields, raising food for their families. They tended the cattle. They spun the wool that later they used to make clothing and bedding.

They made the soap, the candles, and many of the medicines.

Some women shared with their husbands in such occupations as retailing, printmaking, shipbuilding, innkeeping, ferry boat operations, and prison management. They acted as nurses to their communities, as newspaper editors, as teachers. But women were rarely found in such esteemed professions as law and medicine, although no formal education was required for either profession until the end of the eighteenth century. Women who worked outside the home were the exceptions, not the rule.

NATIVE AMERICAN AND BLACK WOMEN

Indian women and black women fared even worse than their white sisters in the early days of American history. The Indian woman

This is the way it was for employed women when America was very young (1750–1815).

Ann Franklin, Benjamin Franklin's sister-in-law, was editor of the Newport, Rhode Island, Mercury (1762).

Mary Salmon of Boston ran a blacksmith's shop where "all gentlemen may have their horses shod in the best manner."

Marguerite Hastner of New York City was a silversmith.

Jane Massey of Charleston, South Carolina, was a gunsmith.

Mary Wilson of Norfolk, Virginia, was a shoemaker.

Mary Katherine Goddard, a Baltimore printer, was authorized by the Continental Congress to print the first copy of the Declaration of Independence with the names of the signers attached.

Anna Zenger, wife of John Peter Zenger, continued to publish her husband's newspaper when he was in jail for publishing an article that opposed the New York colonial government. He was tried in 1735 and acquitted. The case established the principle of a free press.

was considered inferior and an enemy, and the black woman was a slave.

The Indians who met the early Virginia settlers were hostile. But one of them, an Indian Princess named Pocahontas, succeeded in saving the life of Captain John Smith, who had been taken prisoner by Powhatan, her father. Later she married John Rolfe, one of the settlers, who made tobacco a cash crop.

About one-third of the slaves forcibly brought to America were women. Female slaves had no rights. They did field labor on the plantations, performed household duties, raised children, and were often married to slaves. Marriage did not prevent slave women from being separated from their children and husbands.

THE COLONIES REVOLT

During the American Revolution, men and women worked together to create a new nation. Although women generally did not venture onto the fields of battle, there were exceptions to be found among nurses, cooks, and aides. Women in such positions received half of the pay that men did. It is said that in some instances they took over the duties of combat, replacing wounded soldiers.

Once a slave, Phillis Wheatley (1753?–1784) was "snatched" from Africa as a child. She was sold in 1761 to a benevolent Boston family who taught her to read and write, schooled her in the classics, and eventually freed her. Acclaimed by antislavery leaders in Great Britain as well as in the colonies, she was the first black American to publish a book of poetry.

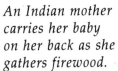

An Indian mother carries her baby on her back as she gathers firewood.

Some wives of Revolutionary War foot soldiers fought alongside their husbands, helping to fire the cannons and perform other battlefield duties.

Lydia Darragh (1729-1789), right. A spy in the American Revolution, she passed secret papers tucked in her needlework about a projected British attack on Philadelphia. General Washington used this information to defeat the British.

Deborah Sampson (1760–1827), lower left. She twice joined the American army using the names Timothy Thayer and Robert Shurtleff. She participated in many raids against the British and their Indian allies. She was seriously wounded.

Abigail Adams (1744–1818), lower right. The wife of John Adams, second U.S. president, and mother of John Quincy Adams, sixth U.S. president, she is remembered as a prolific letter writer and adviser to her husband. In 1985 a stamp was issued commemorating her contribution.

Women of the American Revolution

Betsy Ross (1752–1836), left. She made flags for military units as a profitable sideline. George Washington *never* asked her to make a flag.

Such women as Abigail Adams, Martha Custis Washington, and Mercy Otis Warren gave wise and valuable counsel to their husbands. Another group of women, calling themselves "The Daughters of Liberty," banded together to protest the English taxes on tea and imported fabrics. They protested the English laws under which they were forced to live. They engaged in such activities as making bullets, mending uniforms, and raising crops to feed the army as well as their families.

There are tales of women who acted as spies, bringing information to the revolutionaries that resulted in victories against the British army. So you see, "activism" did not originate in the twentieth century.

It may be said that the upward mobility of women began when they assumed "men's roles." The American Revolution succeeded. A new nation was born.

PRE-CIVIL WAR AMERICANS

In Colonial America the home was the workplace, where families labored side by side to feed, house, and clothe themselves. But the years following the establishment of the new government brought industrialization and the growth of cities, with their factories, mercantile establishments, and a working class.

As men competed in the marketplace to earn money to buy the products that were previously produced at home, the role of middle-class wives was to maintain the home, set an example of virtue and religious piety, and raise their children to be morally upright and industrious.

In the North many poor women, usually young and unmarried and from the farms or newly immigrated from Europe, went to work in the textile mills of New England.

Women in the unindustrialized, agrarian South—whether poor farmers' wives or mistresses of plantations with slaves to do their bidding—were also expected to be virtuous, religious, and devoted to the care of the family.

WOMEN AND THE CIVIL WAR

The Civil War (1861–1865) brought women many new responsibilities but, for some, opportunities as well. While the men fought, women became heads of families and farms, business managers, and income earners. To meet the shortage of nurses, women in both the North and South gave their services. At first there was prejudice against women in nursing, a male occupation. Thousands of women volunteered to assist on the battlefield and in the operating room.

An American household in the early part of the nineteenth century

Mary Boykin Chesnut
(1823–1886) in her diary left us
one of the most vivid accounts
of a Southern woman's daily life
in the mid-nineteenth century.
Daughter of a former governor
of South Carolina and wife of a
senator, she was witness to the
constricted lives of the wellborn
as well as the poor, the rulers
and the slaves.

I have seen a Negro woman sold
upon the block at auction. . . . It
was too dreadful. I tried to reason.
You know how women sell themselves and are sold in marriage, from
queens downwards, eh? You know
what the Bible says about slavery,
and marriage. Poor women, poor
slaves.

Chapter 1

Doctors and Nurses in the Civil War

Elizabeth Blackwell (1821–1910), right. Dr. Blackwell was the first woman to receive a degree in medicine. She pioneered in the training of women army nurses for the North.

Dorothea Dix (1802–1887), left. The superintendent of nurses for the North, she trained women for the army medical corps.

Clara Barton (1821–1912), right. She founded the American Red Cross and raised volunteers for the nursing corps.

Mary Edwards Walker (1832–1919), right. Dr. Walker was the first woman to receive the Congressional Medal of Honor, for her services as a surgeon during the Civil War. She was also a lawyer, teacher, author, and lecturer at the time she received the award in 1865. She pioneered in wearing pantsuits rather than dresses.

The Slave Woman—Another View

Slave women have often been depicted in literature as house servants. Actually, 95 percent of them were fieldworkers who had the same workload as men.

The notion that black women during slavery did kitchen work as a "promotion" from fieldwork was similarly false. Most slave women sought fieldwork to be farther away from white supervision and closer to their families.

Black women protected and encouraged runaway slaves. They often stole food from the household pantry to feed runaways.

*Black slaves planting sweet potatoes on
a South Carolina plantation in 1862*

Chapter 1   ## THE ABOLITIONISTS AND THE TEMPERANCE MOVEMENT

Women of the nineteenth century were at the forefront of the abolitionist cause, the fight against slavery. They helped to organize rallies and participated in the activities of the Underground Railroad in spiriting escaping slaves away to safe refuge. They spoke out against the evils of slavery, as a degradation not only of the enslaved but of the slaveowner as well.

One of the Underground Railroad's most celebrated "conductors" was Harriet Tubman, a black woman, who led more than three hundred slaves to freedom.

Women also spoke out against alcohol, for high alcohol consumption throughout the nation was widespread. It often led to broken homes, and wives and children were left without any means of support.

Some of the women who labored the hardest to free the slaves and to secure the accepted family structure went on to lead the fight for women's suffrage. They had worked hard to secure the rights of others, believing that male leaders in the abolition and temperance movements would in turn support women's rights. That such was not the case became evident when in 1870 black men were granted suffrage under the Fifteenth Amendment, but women were still denied the right to vote. Women came to realize that

though their cause was just, the battle was just beginning.

GO WEST, YOUNG WOMAN

Many women who made the long, dangerous journey west in the covered wagons of the nineteenth century did so for the freedom that frontier life offered.

Again and again, they faced challenges without any conveniences. They carved a civilization out of a barren, often hostile, environment. They stood shoulder to shoulder with men, and they were valued as individuals.

It is no coincidence that the first states to grant women the right to vote were western territories at the time: Wyoming in 1869 and Utah in 1870.

Pioneering women also found more freedom to do what they wanted. For some, this was finding a suitable husband; for others it was becoming teachers, army wives, missionaries, homesteaders, even miners and boardinghouse managers.

The hardships of pioneer life continued, in a far lesser form, even into the twentieth century. Although they were not faced with physical dangers, women in these new states had to face the same hardships and lack of conveniences as their pioneer sisters. They too not only survived but raised large families and worked toward gaining political recognition.

Above: a family in front of their sod house on the Kansas prairie in the early 1890s. Below: pioneer woman gathering buffalo chips to be used as a source of heat.

In a massive demonstration for women's suffrage, five thousand women marched up Pennsylvania Avenue in Washington, D.C., March 3, 1913, the day before Woodrow Wilson was inaugurated as president. Police stood by as the marchers were attacked by hostile onlookers.

C H A P T E R   2

WOMEN ORGANIZE

"If I had had the slightest premonition of all that was to follow . . . I fear I should not have had the courage to risk it," Elizabeth Cady Stanton wrote in her memoirs, looking back at that first "Woman's Rights Convention" held in Seneca Falls, New York, in 1848.

For those women who first joined together to fight against sex discrimination, it was a long and uphill battle. It meant defiance of laws and customs that had been accepted from the time of the first settlements.

What were these "discriminations"?

Women were not permitted to speak at public meetings.

Women were denied the right to vote.

Women could not attend male colleges.

Women did not have a free choice of courses or education.

Women could not keep ownership of property when they married.

In addition:

Women were discriminated against in public and private employment because of sex, race, color, religion, national origin, and age.

Women could be beaten legally by their "overlords"—their husbands.

Women were generally expected to be "seen but not heard."

Women found that they faced unequal pay for the same jobs that men performed.

Chapter 2 **THE BEGINNING**

On July 19 and 20, 1848, three hundred people came together at Seneca Falls, New York, to discuss and resolve the inequities that had made women second-class citizens. Those women who had accepted their positions as standing "behind their men" now demanded the right to stand "alongside" their mates—alongside men in general. At this convention emerged one of the greatest organizers in the fight for equal rights, Susan B. Anthony, and one of its greatest speakers, Elizabeth Cady Stanton.

It was Stanton who used the Declaration of Independence as a model when she drafted the convention's Resolutions, beginning, "We hold these truths to be self-evident: that all men and women are created equal. . . . "

This historic meeting was but the beginning of a fight that would go on for years, bringing ridicule and scorn down upon the heads of those who were in the forefront and also those who followed, extracting a heavy toll on the health and comfort of the determined women.

Many women joined in the fight—picketing, protesting, parading, campaigning—demanding that women be given the same rights as men had. One of the most forceful speakers for the movement was a freed black slave, Sojourner Truth, who had been active in aiding slaves to escape from their bondage in the South.

Seventy-two years elapsed between the time of the Seneca Falls convention and the passage of the Nineteenth Amendment in 1920, which gave the vote to women. Only one woman who had attended that first convention lived to cast her ballot.

Sojourner Truth was an electrifying speaker who spoke out passionately for women's rights.

22

This 1901 parody reflects the mood of the country at the time: if women were granted more rights, men would be reduced to doing the household chores.

Opposition to granting women the right to vote was strong.

STAND BY THE WOMEN

WOMAN'S RIGHT IS THE RIGHT OF FREEDOM FROM POLITICAL DUTIES

VOTE NO ON WOMAN SUFFRAGE NOV. 2

N. Y. STATE ASSOCIATION OPPOSED TO WOMAN SUFFRAGE
37 W. 39th ST., NEW YORK

Chapter 2

Pioneers of the Women's Movement

Lucretia Mott (1793–1880) was an early advocate of equal rights for women. A Quaker minister and a gifted speaker, she was highly respected for her original, independent thinking.

Elizabeth Cady Stanton (1815–1902) was called the "mother of the women's suffrage movement." She organized the Woman's Rights Convention of 1848. She was a leader in the fight for women's rights to own property and for divorce laws more favorable to women.

Lucy Stone (1818–1893) set a precedent for professional women's use of their maiden names. Lucy Stone and Henry Blackwell (brother of the country's first female doctor, Elizabeth Blackwell) were married in 1855. They did not use the word *obey* in their marriage ceremony. She was the first woman in Massachusetts to earn a college degree.

Susan Brownell Anthony (1820–1906) was both a woman suffrage leader and a social reformer. She was raised as a Quaker and became a schoolteacher. She left education to devote her efforts to the temperance movement (against alcohol) and the abolition cause (against slavery). She attempted to have a provision inserted into the Fourteenth Amendment to grant the right to vote to women as well as to male blacks, and she was arrested when she attempted to vote in Rochester, New York, local elections. Susan B. Anthony built the women's rights movement into a national organization.

Carrie Chapman Catt (1859–1947) was an ardent supporter of women's right to vote. She succeeded Susan Anthony as president of the National American Woman Suffrage Association (NAWSA), and in the twentieth century she worked for individual states to give women the vote.

Victoria Woodhull (1838–1927) fought for women's freedom in the economy—on Wall Street, in Congress, and in the White House. She was the first of many feminists to appear before Congress to plead for and demand the rights of American women.

25

C H A P T E R   3

"A WOMAN'S PLACE"

The passage of the Nineteenth Amendment gave women the right to vote but little else. With discriminatory laws and accustomed ways of perceiving women's role in society, women still had a long way to go. Some of their gains can be attributed to outside factors.

MECHANICAL LIBERATION: ITS IMPACT ON THE WORLD OF YOUR GRANDPARENTS, PARENTS, AND YOU

It has been said that the only thing that is permanent is *change*. Looking around the average American home today, the first thing we notice is that everything is convenient. How cool it is in the summer, thanks to the air conditioner. How well our foods keep in those efficient refrigerators. How simple it is to take care of loads and loads of soiled clothing in our washers and dryers. What a boon it is to defrost our frozen dinners in those microwave ovens. We can push a button and make almost anything happen. How things have changed! Our grandmothers and great grandmothers were the first to liberate themselves from household chores that took hours and hours to accomplish, and they had few appliances but vacuum cleaners and electric irons to aid them. Think what they could have done with a dishwasher!

The roles of mothers and grandmothers are now more noticeably different from household and family duties and responsibilities of the past. Formerly, most women's lives were exclusively centered on the home and child-

Mother and children

This photograph appeared in Leslie's Weekly magazine of May 17, 1906. The caption reads: "Good housewives of the future—girl pupils at a Cincinnati suburban high school learning the art of cooking."

An early twentieth century advertisement for a vacuum cleaner. The caption reads: "Mrs. Bliss was a little slow to take to electrical appliances. But she is using them one by one and the vacuum cleaner has become a member of the family."

The supermarket of today, with its wealth of convenience foods and its electronically-read pricing codes, is far removed from the simpler food stores of the first half of the twentieth century.

raising. Women are now freer, in part because of the mechanical and technological revolutions that have taken place in the home. Women are no longer "servants and machines." Kitchen gadgets and household conveniences are available. These permit more leisure, less arduous household duties, and opportunities to participate in social and political activities and to seek employment outside the home. Women's lives have been affected by the rapid advances in industry, changes in the consumer and service sectors, and the communications and transportation revolutions.

When women shopped in the early twentieth century, it meant going from store to store, from neighborhood to neighborhood (but believe it or not, most of the purchases could be delivered—at no extra cost). Later, convenience stores and markets, as well as shopping centers, lessened the burdens of marketing. Methods of preserving and distributing vegetables, fruits, meats, and essentials, plus the concentration of those essentials in fewer stores reduced the chores of housewives. The new Main Street of America is frequently the multi-storied, climate-controlled, landscaped shopping mall. Liberation from the traditional roles, time-consuming and wearisome, has fostered a new way of life.

Chapter 3

THE "LIBERATED WOMAN"

Today parents and grandparents, teachers and ministers express shock at the way young people behave. So it was when they were growing up. Young women, then and now, exhibited a revolution in manners and morals. In the "roaring twenties" there emerged the flamboyant, defiant, and independent young woman—the "flapper." She was usually a working girl who used makeup, had short, black-dyed hair, smoked cigarettes and drank alcohol, and wore necklaces and bracelets and skimpy dresses. This description did not typify American women as a whole. Some expressed sentiments such as "come out of the kitchen," "careers instead of housewives," and "more child care and support services."

American society did not readily accommodate women who wanted to combine the role of wife–mother with a career. For the most part, mothers and grandmothers received little help from professional schools, employers, co-workers, child-care personnel, husbands, and friends and relatives. If they sought careers, they were in "women's fields"—retailing, fashion, teaching, social work, nursing, and women's medical specialties such as gynecology and pediatrics.

*A typical
1920s flapper*

30

Peeling apples to make an apple pie

THE "TYPICAL HOUSEWIFE"

Two world wars gave women the opportunity to fill nontraditional roles, but this opportunity did not last. At the end of World War I and again at the end of World War II, women who had held jobs previously held by men returned to marriage and homemaking. The young married families of the 1950s moved out of the small towns and large cities into the suburbs. By the mid-1970s, 40 percent of the American population were living in the suburbs.

The wives of blue-collar workers and low-income white-collar workers for the most part depended on marriage to provide them with economic security. Working-class men tended to support their wives and children on their factory and clerical salaries. When the income was inadequate, some wives took jobs to supplement their family incomes.

BABY BOOMERS

The "baby boom generation"—men and women born in the 1940s, 1950s, and 1960s—used wheels instead of feet, credit cards instead of cash. In many cities and communities "downtown" had lost its heart because the automobile made shopping centers and

Chapter 3

shopping malls available to women. More than forty-seven hundred new shopping malls had appeared around the country by the 1980s. The shopping malls were directed chiefly at the white middle-class shopper. Gone are the small tailoring, shoe repair, and grocery stores—all cheap service establishments used formerly by your grandparents and great grandparents. The result: more variety, time saving, less arduous chores. While women without automobiles were trapped in their homes all day, the suburban woman with a car often spent a large part of her time behind the wheel—driving husband back and forth to the railroad station, going to the supermarket, driving the children to and from school, to scout meetings, and music lessons. A woman could easily spend twenty hours a week behind the wheel—half of the work hours of a salaried employee.

Americans continue to move about the country seeking new employment opportunities and ways of life. Most American women live in or near a city. The average woman will not stay in one place all of her life; she will move from five to seven times in her lifetime.

Changes are still in the making. Now that we have added the computer as a tool for the home homemakers can order goods, maintain their bank accounts, provide entertainment and learning for themselves and their children, and be linked up to libraries and computer networks of electronic data banks. With the availability of such electronic devices, women can use their homes for their offices or base for employment, thus giving them greater flexibility and freedom.

This is the time for society to accept the inevitable—there is nothing so permanent as *change*.

CHAPTER 4

FIRST-CLASS CITIZENS?

Abigail Adams, wife of the Massachusetts delegate to the Continental Congress, stayed home, ran the family business, raised her children, and made it possible for her husband, John, to lead in the fight for independence from Great Britain. In her letters she constantly reminded John to "remember the ladies." Her warning continued to remind the men who were writing the Constitution that women would not feel themselves bound by laws that would give them no voice or representation.

Imagine how amazed John Adams would have been to learn that a woman had been a candidate for vice-president in 1984. Geraldine Ferraro changed politics, forever.

RIGHTS NOT EASILY WON

Ask yourself a question. What is meant by "women's rights" today?

The right to vote
The right to own property
The right to credit
The right to join the armed forces
The right to seek election to high office
The right to serve on juries in civil and criminal cases

These are rights many of us take for granted today. But these are rights recently won.

Women got the right to vote in 1920. Some women's organizations, such as the National American Woman Suffrage Association (NAWSA), ended their activities. But sex discrimination continued to permeate almost every sphere of human endeavor. Alice Paul and her National Woman's Party began to push for a constitutional amendment that would abolish *all* legal discrimination whether or not it favored women.

33

Chapter 4

THE EQUAL RIGHTS AMENDMENT

Equality of rights under the law shall not be denied or abridged by the United States or by any State on account of sex.

The battle for the Equal Rights Amendment (ERA) has been waged since 1923. Finally, in 1972, both houses of Congress approved ERA. Three-fourths of the states and *not* the president have to approve the amendment. The amendment was endorsed by Presidents Eisenhower, Kennedy, Johnson, Nixon, Ford, and Carter, but not President Reagan.

Constitutional amendments must be ratified by either "the legislatures in three-fourths of the several states or by conventions in three-fourths thereof." The ERA traveled the more common route: it was approved by two-thirds of both houses of Congress and submitted for ratification to the legislatures in the states. Congress originally set seven years for the ratification of ERA by the required thirty-eight states. When ERA failed to obtain approval, Congress granted a three-year extension. The amendment was defeated June 30, 1982, when the time for ratification expired. Women's rights advocates were unable to persuade the required number of state legislatures to ratify the amendment.

Phyllis Schafley led conservative men and women of both political parties in opposing ERA.

Conservative religious groups, such as fundamentalists and Mormons, together with antiabortion groups, which had the support of the Roman Catholic Church, worked to defeat ERA. They were joined by such political groups as the John Birch Society and the American Party.

Extensive media campaigns, lobbying, and threats of boycotts of states that did not ratify ERA did not succeed. The amendment was reintroduced in Congress shortly after its defeat.

It took seventy years for women to get the right to vote. For almost another seventy years since that time, women have been trying to be included among those covered by the United States Constitution. No end to the struggle is in sight.

AN INFORMED ELECTORATE

With the passage of the Nineteenth Amendment in 1920, a nonpartisan organization called the League of Women Voters was formed. Its purpose? To promote "political responsibility through informed and active participation of citizens in government."

Since the league's founding, its members have studied issues, lobbied for political reform, and sponsored public debate on matters relating to government, including, in recent years, the nationally televised presidential debates. Membership today is approximately 200,000.

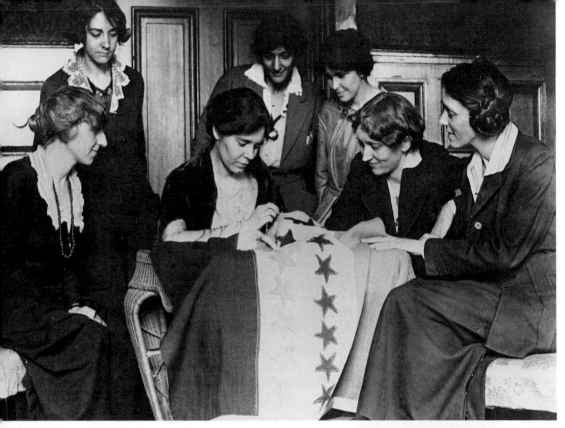

Alice Paul and her National Woman's Party proposed and fought for an Equal Rights Amendment as early as 1923. She is shown here sewing another star on the party's flag, indicating that one more state ratified the proposed amendment. In the end, not enough states ratified the amendment to bring it into law.

Above: Ella Baker (1903-1986), a social activist, organized consumer cooperatives, recruited members for the NAACP, and was a driving force behind the Student Nonviolent Coordinating Committee (SNCC). Left: in the 1970s and 1980s the fight for passage of the Equal Rights Amendment gained new impetus. Here women march up the Avenue of the Americas in New York City in support of the amenament.

WOMEN IN THE COURTROOM

Women have long been discriminated against within the walls of the courtroom—as jurors, judges, and lawyers. Not until 1950 did Congress enact legislation that made all women eligible to sit on federal juries. In 1975, the Supreme Court, in clarifying a decision that struck down a Louisiana law excluding women from juries, held that juries must be selected from a pool drawn from a representative cross-section of the community.

Significant progress has been made in women's fight to enter the legal profession. From 1973 to 1986, the number of women who practiced law in the United States increased nearly tenfold—from 12,000 to 116,000. And from 1976 to 1986, the proportion of women in law schools rose from 4 percent to over 40 percent. If this trend continues, by the beginning of the year 2000 half of all lawyers in America will be women.

The number of women judges is on the increase, too. In 1971 there were fewer than two hundred. By 1980, the number had nearly tripled.

WOMEN IN POLITICS

In the nineteenth century the western states took the initiative in granting women political recognition. Wyoming, in 1890, was the first state to grant women the right to vote. Utah, Colorado, and Idaho followed very shortly. At the local level, Argonia, Kansas, elected the first woman mayor in the United States, in 1887. Also in Kansas, in the following year, the five seats on the town council as well as the office of mayor of Oskaloosa were filled by women. Among other "firsts" was Wyoming's woman governor, Nellie Tayloe Ross, elected in 1925. She later became the first woman director of the U.S. mint.

There was no great flood of women into the U.S. House of Representatives immediately following the enactment of the Nineteenth Amendment. However, in 1916 Montana elected Jeanette Rankin to the House. And by the 1950s thirty women had been elected to the House of Representatives. The first women senators were appointed to succeed their deceased husbands.

Changes and acceptance come slowly. But the proportion of women in state legislatures tripled between 1972 and 1983 and continues to rise. The number of cities with a population of more than thirty thousand that had women mayors increased from seven to almost one hundred. At the national level, the first female presidential cabinet appointment was Frances Perkins, secretary of labor from 1933 to 1945. Since that time, others have followed, including Elizabeth Dole, the secretary of transportation; Margaret

Jeannette Rankin (1880-1973), an active feminist, was the first woman to be elected to Congress. During her first term in office, she opposed U.S. entry into into World War I. In 1940 she was elected to a second term, and the following year she was the only member of Congress to vote against our entry into World War II.

Women as judges are no longer looked upon as a curiosity.

Women in government (clockwise from upper left): Council President Carol Bellamy of New York City; U.S. Representative Claudine Schneider of Rhode Island; Governor Madeleine Kunin of Vermont; Supreme Court Justice Sandra Day O'Connor; U.S. Senator Nancy Kassebaum of Kansas.

Shirley Chisholm was the first black woman in the House of Representatives. In 1972, she ran for the presidency of the United States, and won 10 percent of the Democratic Convention votes.

Heckler, secretary of health and human services, and the "landmark" appointment of Sandra Day O'Connor as the first woman justice of the Supreme Court.

The emergence of women as political power brokers is reflected in the National Women's Political Caucus, a bipartisan group of Democratic and Republican women who have sought to increase the number of female delegates to national political nominating conventions. They have advocated active participation in the formulation of party platforms to represent more adequately the concerns of women and children. They seek to encourage more women to enter national politics as candidates.

Just where are women in federal, state, and local governments today? Everywhere. From city councils to state legislatures to governors' offices, Congress, Senate, presidential cabinets, and the Supreme Court—and, almost, the vice-presidency.

And what have they achieved? Almost all women's legislation has been introduced and shepherded through Congress by women, including the ERA, the Equal Pay Act, battered spouse legislation, the Rape Privacy Act, and the Displaced Homemakers Act.

In the elections of 1986, seventy-nine women ran for Congress or governor, a record number in U.S. history. One-third won. The women's vote in 1986 helped the Democratic party regain control of the U.S. Senate; an ABC-TV poll after the elections found that 57 percent of the women who voted, voted Democratic.

CHAPTER 5

GETTING AN EDUCATION

"Why," asked Professor Higgins in the musical comedy *My Fair Lady*, "can't a woman be more like a man?" Well, Professor Higgins, because men wouldn't let them. One important way that women were kept from being more like men was that women did not have access to the education they needed to prove themselves equal to men.

In colonial days women were not given the same education as were men. It seemed sufficient that they be prepared for marriage and homemaking—"a woman's place was in the home." At that time parents were responsible for the education of their children. Massachusetts required that every town have a public school, but the education of girls ceased after grammar school. Men went on to higher education.

It was not until the early 1800s that girls had access to pri-

vate secondary schools, known as seminaries. In 1824 the first public high school for girls was opened in Worcester, Massachusetts.

As the number of these schools increased, it became apparent that high school education should be available to all boys and girls. This became the responsibility of each individual state. The result is that each of the fifty states has a separate system of education, with a department of education at the federal level that aids and advises in their operations. Sex-segregated public schools have almost vanished in the United States.

WOMEN BREAK THE EDUCATIONAL BARRIERS

Once the matter of women's access to education beyond the ele-

*The graduating class of 1884
at Radcliffe College*

mentary grades was settled, there began the long, painful, and frustrating battle for admission into college. It was considered proper for women with only a high school education to teach, but men were required to have a college degree—hence, women were paid less than men. And since women were not admitted into high academic training facilities, they were barred from entering such professions as medicine, science, and law throughout the early nineteenth century.

In 1837 Oberlin College finally accepted applications from women, both white and black. Women were on their way! But it was not until the Civil War and after that other colleges, exclusively for women, opened. Among them there were five notable names that maintain their excellence today: Vassar, Smith, Wellesley, Radcliffe, and Bryn Mawr. These private colleges for women now accept male students, as Yale and Harvard now accept women—a far cry from the discriminatory practices of the nineteenth and part of the twentieth century.

Another interesting factor that contributed to differences in educational training of women was that many colleges created "a homey atmosphere" for their women students. They felt that they should emphasize femininity. But Bryn Mawr felt differently. Its president, M. Carey Thomas, rejected any hint of domesticity or

gender differentiation and insisted that there be no architectural differences between men's and women's houses. She once said that there could be no difference between instructions given to bridge builders simply because one wore a skirt and one wore pants. Today most colleges are dedicated to that philosophy of equality of educational opportunities, leading to equality of degrees.

Women now receive degrees in all of the fields once exclusively reserved for male students. Nevertheless, although women are in a majority in the teaching profession, this pertains only to the elementary grades. In colleges and universities the faculties are overwhelmingly male.

But important changes are occurring. The percentage of women who earn Ph.D.'s has increased dramatically. This has opened the doors to degrees in medicine, executive business positions, law, hospital administration, dentistry, science research, engineering, and many other formerly all-male provinces. Women astronauts have earned their status through advanced degrees in highly complicated fields at the same level as their male counterparts.

Individual girls have challenged school policies that denied them the right to take shop courses or that forced them to study home economics. It was a New York City girl who forced the board of education to desegre-

In this Kansas State University classroom in the early 1900s, "coeds" learn to sew.

Today more girls are taking shop courses.

43

Chapter 5

Christa McAuliffe was chosen from eleven thousand applicants to be the first teacher in space. McAuliffe taught high school social studies in Concord, New Hampshire. On January 28, 1986, she was killed when the space shuttle *Challenger* exploded 74 seconds after liftoff. Among the six other astronauts killed in the explosion was mission specialist Judith Resnik, who held a Ph.D. in electrical engineering.

Therese (Terry) Dozier won the teaching profession's highest honor in 1985 when she was named National Teacher of the Year. Abandoned in Vietnam as a child, she was adopted by an American couple and brought to the United States. She won scholarships to the University of Florida, where she graduated with a straight-A average. She teaches history in Columbia, South Carolina.

Sally Ride, the first woman astronaut, has spoken at educational meetings throughout the United States. A central theme in her talks with science teachers is that they must not forget the girls, that they must consciously encourage their female students to pursue academic excellence in science. Ride came from an all-girl high school and credits her teachers with the inspiration to pursue a career in the sciences.

gate Stuyvesant High School, a highly regarded all-male science school. Fewer books on the history of the United States are written in a gender-specific manner, detailing only male accomplishments.

At one time it was not unusual to hear the question "Would you feel comfortable with a woman doctor?" Today the question seems rather silly. As a matter of fact, the number of women physicians, dentists, and related practitioners increased by 100 percent during the 1970s, and it is predicted that the trend will continue.

Just consider these statistics:

In 1970, 699 women graduated from medical school, and 801 women graduated from law school.

In 1981, 3,833 women graduated from medical school, and 11,768 women graduated from law school.

And the number of women who earned business degrees has increased 700 percent from 1975 to 1985.

TRAVELING THE LONG ROAD

College enrollment is about the same for both sexes. From 1950 to 1980 the proportion of female college graduates more than doubled. Nevertheless, women earned fewer professional and graduate degrees.

The classroom climate for college women in the 1980s leaves much to be desired. The Association of American Colleges' Project on the "Status and Education of Women" reported in 1984 thirty ways in which female students are treated differently from male students in the classroom. Here are a few examples:

Women are interrupted more often than men.

Men get more eye contact.

Women are less likely to be called on, even when they raise their hands.

Professors are less likely to engage in dialogue with a female student when she makes a point.

Students know more about science in the 1980s, but boys still do better than girls. Here are some findings from a 1983 School Children's Science Knowledge and Skills Survey, as reported by Teachers College, Columbia University:

A gap exists between boys and girls in science achievement.

More women are pursuing formerly male dominated careers in science.

Attempts have been made to improve educational opportunities for girls.

Differences were greater in the physical sciences than in biology.

Girls did best on biology subjects.

Gender gaps appeared in science test questions given to fifth-graders, ninth-graders, and a general science and physics test given to twelfth-graders. Differences between boys' and girls' abilities widened as grade levels rose. Scores on physics tests, however, showed the smallest gender differences. (The testers speculated that only the abler female students took twelfth-grade physics.)

Some suggestions for improving female scores:

Girls should be given "hands on" experience in handling physical and concrete materials, together with more laboratory experiences.

There should be more female instructors in the sciences.

In the conclusion to the survey, the researchers stated:

We're disappointed that there hasn't been more progress in closing the gap between males and females. Unless this difference is reversed, the United States will be unable to meet its 1995 goal of providing the finest level of mathematics, science and technology education in the world.

Mary Wollstonecraft, the eighteenth-century English author of *A Vindication of the Rights of Women*, once declared, "I don't want women to have power over males, but over themselves." This is the position that today's women have taken in their battle for equality in education. Young women today can feel confident that the future of women in education has become secure, that they will be considered as qualified to fill all of the formerly all-male positions. From college presidents to department heads, women have proved their right to be considered on the same level as those men who are usually on the "preferred list."

Above: a math student studying calculus. Below: an Oberlin College student in 1986, working in the chemistry lab.

C H A P T E R 6

A PART OF THE WORK FORCE

Few women who worked outside the home in the 1800s posed any threat to men in competing for jobs. They were the schoolteachers, seamstresses, domestics. Textile mills also employed women, but in heavy industry only men were hired. Before the 1870s most women had no choice but to depend on men for their livelihood.

As for new immigrants and free black women, their jobs were mainly as housekeepers, factory workers, or nursemaids. The hours were long and the pay low. There was little privacy and less leisure.

With the coming of the industrial revolution and its need for a large labor force, more women sought employment outside the home. By 1890 there were more than 4 million women in the work force, in such occupations as sewing, tailoring, shoemaking, print-

ing, textile manufacturing, and even cigar making. There were also houseworkers, laundresses, nursemaids, and hospital attendants. Wages were deplorably low, with no means for women to change the conditions that had been imposed.

Then came the fire at the Triangle Shirtwaist Company in New York City in 1911. In this tragic event 146 workers, most of them women and children, jumped to their deaths or died behind the factory's locked doors. In this part of the garment industry, women's wages were from three to five dollars per week—one-half of men's wages in the same industry.

What followed was really revolutionary. Two women, Mary Drier and her sister Margaret Drier Robbins, of the New York branch of the National Woman's Trade Union, began to organize

One witness to the Triangle Shirtwaist Company fire was Frances Perkins, who later recalled the horror of seeing "young women poised on window ledges in attitudes of prayer before they jumped to their deaths." An active campaigner for improved conditions for workers, Perkins went on to become secretary of labor during the administration of Franklin D. Roosevelt. She was the chief architect of our social security system.

A Part of the Work Force

Women at work in a textile factory at the turn of the century

women workers in other cities. Some gains were made. This union eventually merged with the International Ladies' Garment Workers Union (ILGWU).

LABOR UNIONS

Why did women seek the protection of unions? They had good reason to. Their working conditions were miserable; their hours were long. They were forced to take positions that men had rejected, at wages much lower than those of men. They had to combine work and homemaking, which meant that often children were neglected and deprived.

Realizing that women were moving up in the labor force and that women were the largest segment of unorganized workers, the American Federation of Labor (AFL) and the Congress of Industrial Organizations (CIO) began to solicit women as members. Many independent unions also joined in this movement to organize women into groups. Eventually the ILGWU became a part of the AFL-CIO, and as the membership of the ILGWU swelled, it came to exert great power in what had been a union of highly skilled workers, most of whose members had been exclusively male.

OFFICE WORKERS

Women in so-called white-collar jobs were not much better off than their blue-collar sisters. The

typewriter and the telephone were called women's machines, just as the loom and the sewing machine had been. Indeed, the buyers of the shirtwaists made in such "sweat shops" as the Triangle Shirtwaist Company were schoolteachers, secretaries, and sales clerks. The shirtwaist (blouse), worn with a rather plain black skirt, was the "uniform" of the white-collar working woman.

As women moved into low-paying positions as file clerks, typists, and secretaries, men held the power in managerial positions.

ROSIE THE RIVETER

It took a world war to give American women the opportunity to show they could handle jobs formerly available only to men. When the United States went to war against Germany and Japan in December of 1941, workers were needed to fill the jobs vacated by those who joined the military. Family life was temporarily changed, as the "little woman" traded her apron for coveralls to work in a munitions factory. Women became welders, machinists, and truck drivers or took other jobs that had always been considered "men's work." The shift of women to traditionally male jobs indicates how quickly social and economic changes can take place. The mobility of women to industry was made possible when peoples' attitudes supported it.

*Left: early twentieth
century telephone
operators with
their supervisors.
Below: a department
store supervisor
and his female staff
in the dry-goods
department.*

Left: Waves (Women Accepted for Voluntary Emergency Service) working on the engine of a Navy scout trainer in 1943. Both were aviation metalsmiths, third class, graduates of the Navy's Technical Training Center at Norman, Oklahoma. Below: welders at the General Aircraft Corporation's Long Island City plant in October 1943. They are using their lunch hour to discuss labor negotiation problems. Facing page: rivetgun in hand, a factory worker helps assemble a World War II fighter plane at the Lockheed Aircraft plant in Burbank, California.

Chapter 6 **LIFE RETURNS TO "NORMAL"**

After World War II, there were massive layoffs as the need for wartime production ended. The returning men were no longer soldiers but veterans, who claimed their rights to the jobs they had been forced to leave. But the women who had replaced them had found that not only could they perform as well as the men, but they were enjoying their salaries, too!

The readjustment in the households created many problems. Wives were not eager to return to their dull tasks, and many of them accepted lower-paying jobs in industry, often for no other reason than to "stay out of the kitchen." Sharing of household responsibilities had its beginning in this decision.

To cite some figures and facts as the result of World War II:

More than 6 million women went to work for the first time.

The number of women in the work force increased from 25 percent in 1940 to 36 percent in 1945.

In 1945 the United States had the highest divorce rate in the world, 31 divorces for every 100 marriages, double the pre-World War II rate.

The American family would never be the same again. Though many women returned to the role of homemaker, the seeds of a cultural revolution had been sown, and the traditional family structure, although seemingly in place, was slowly breaking down.

Women who chose to remain in the labor force after World War II often found their jobs no longer available to them. Thousands were fired to make way for returning veterans. Many found themselves relegated again to low-paying "feminine" jobs such as secretary or file clerk.

Those who returned to being housewives were also soon mothers. The "baby boom" was on, and the family station wagon became the symbol of the ideal American family. The split-level house in the tree-shaded suburbs was the workplace for the middle-class woman now.

A QUIET REVOLUTION

Slowly, more and more women began to return to jobs outside the home. Those that were open to them were still the traditional female jobs, low paying and unchallenging. But legislation generated by the civil rights movement of the 1960s and 1970s opened up new opportunities for employment, and women began to move into traditionally blue-collar, male-dominated fields, such as mining and heavy industry.

54

Olivia Rowe, one of the first female coal miners, is shown here in 1974, working 500–1,000 feet (150–305 m) underground near Johnstown, Pennsylvania.

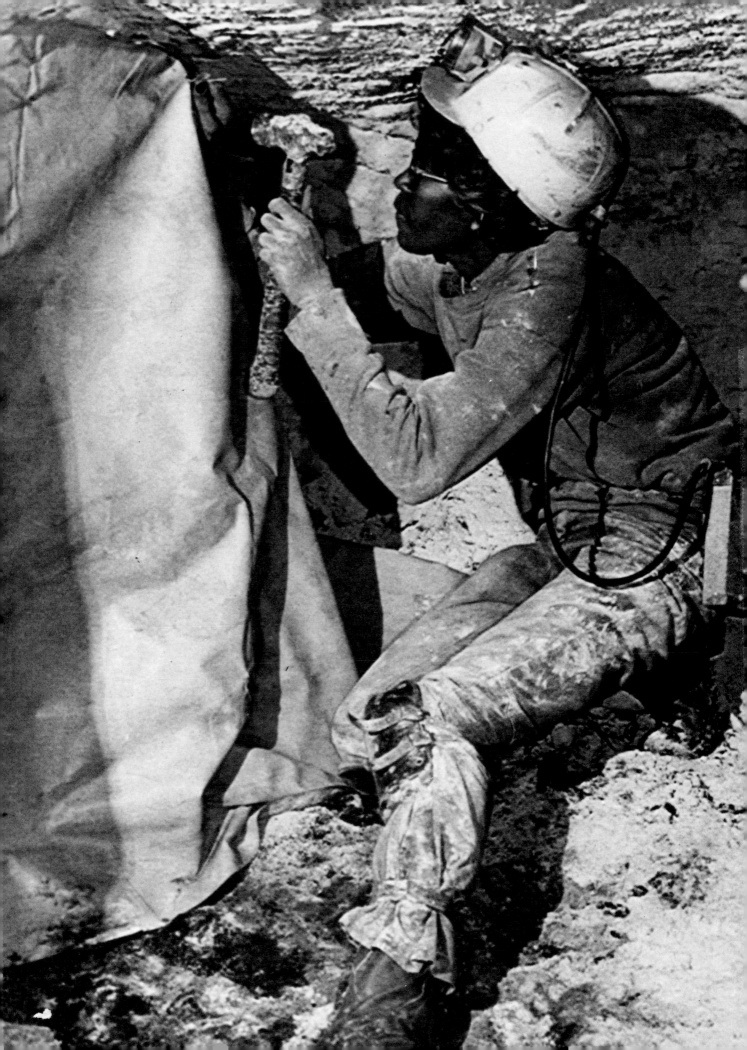

Chapter 6

A Puerto Rican woman, Felicia Rincon de Gautier, combined both a business and a political career. Rising from the slums, she built a successful dress business and became mayor of San Juan, Puerto Rico. During both careers, she emphasized the need to employ women.

Neale S. Godfrey, president and chief executive officer of The First Women's Bank, New York, came to her new position in 1985 after serving as a vice president with Chase Manhattan Bank for thirteen years.

At The First Women's Bank, while awaiting the birth of her second child, she managed the bank from her home, spending four to five hours a day on the telephone conferring with staff and overseeing the bank's operations.

Sylvia Porter, through her syndicated newspaper column, has advised millions of Americans on how to manage their money. She was named one of America's Twenty-five Most Influential Women by the *World Almanac* and Woman of the Decade by the *Ladies Home Journal*.

Women began to make inroads in white-collar positions as well, moving into managerial roles that brought higher salaries and a greater sense of achievement.

Nineteen eighty-six was the first year in which women held the majority of professional jobs in the United States. It was a historic milestone for working women. Although men continue to dominate such prestigious fields as medicine and law, there are now more women psychologists, statisticians, reporters, and editors.

According to Harvard labor economist David E. Bloom, "The growing number of women in the labor market . . . is probably the most important development in the American labor market that has ever taken place."

Labor statistics show, however, that in spite of advances, there is still an earning gap. At the end of 1985, the median weekly earnings for professional men were $581, compared with $419 for professional women.

WOMEN IN FINANCE

The number of women who work on Wall Street increased tremendously between 1975 and 1985, but few women rose to *high* executive positions. For example, in 1985 at E. F. Hutton, one of the large Wall Street firms, of the twenty-nine first vice-presidents in "deal-making roles," just six were women.

In 1983 Columbia University School of Business reported 38 percent of its graduating class was female, compared with 5 percent in 1972.

The book *The Managerial Woman*, by Margaret Hennig and Anne Jardim, explored the impact of women entering male business areas in 1977. They found that women were beginning to make their presence felt.

WOMEN IN THE MILITARY

When choosing a career, many women today join the armed forces. Registration is not required of women at eighteen as it is of men, but all of the military service institutions accept women applicants. They train women to meet their standards, not relaxing any of the requirements because of gender. Those women who cannot "take it" are eliminated on the same basis as are men. Only one restriction remains. Women cannot be sent into combat. As nurses, however, they do go into combat zones.

Once utilized only to meet personnel shortages, women are now permitted to qualify for promotion to high rank, as commanding officers of noncombat units. Motherhood and military careers have been combined, and the armed services have even provided maternity apparel.

Women in the Armed Forces

1972:   Less than 2 percent of officers and enlisted personnel were women.

1985:   Approximately 9.5 percent of officers and enlisted personnel were women.

Female officers: 28,719
Male officers: 303,000

Enlisted women: 172,941
Enlisted men: 1,834,000

Warrant Officer Maxine Bond picks up her three-year-old daughter Bridget at the child care center at Peterson Air Force Base in Colorado.

Thousands of women volunteered to serve with the army in Vietnam. These women, often in their early twenties and many fresh out of training schools, were medical assistants and nurses. Since this was not a "declared war," they were not barred from combat zones, and many of them were in danger equal to that of the soldiers in the fields of operation.

Women are prohibited by law from serving in navy and air force units that could expose them to combat. The army's policy also excludes women from these assignments. They are prohibited from holding jobs that might result in direct confrontation with the enemy—hand-to-hand, rifle-to-rifle contact. Women, however, may serve in units that support combat troops. Women command noncombat units, head multimillion-dollar procurement offices, and lead intelligence forces.

However, combat duty is a requirement for many military promotions—thus, another barrier for women.

WOMEN IN THE CLERGY

Standing in the pulpit, an ordained member of the clergy, delivering a sermon? A woman? What once seemed highly unlikely is now becoming more accepted.

For centuries women were barred from the clergy, except perhaps in the Quaker religion. Before the Civil War (1861–1865), one woman, Antoinette Brown Blackwell, served as pastor of a Protestant church, although she was refused a minister's license because of her sex. Blackwell was well known as both an effective speaker and a person of sterling qualities. However, women were not readily accepted into the ministries of any religious group with any enthusiasm. Even today they are considered somewhat as curiosities, and the Roman Catholic Church continues to deny priesthood to women. In spite of the resistance, women are entering schools of religious training in greater and greater numbers.

CHAPTER 7

ACHIEVERS ALL

A vast number of intelligent, idealistic, able, and ambitious women made a tremendous effort to make a place for themselves in America and the world. Their efforts produced results despite existing barriers. Their extraordinary accomplishments have enhanced the worlds of arts and letters, humanities, science and technology, entertainment, competitive sports, communications—all facets of life.

WOMEN IN THE ARTS

It has been said that Anonymous was a woman. Before the twentieth century, few women painters were recognized for their accomplishments, and those who were often felt compelled to restrict their subject matter to domestic scenes—mothers and children, pets, fruit on the table, noncontroversial subjects. Colonial women channeled their talents into the creation of exquisite crochetwork, patterned quilts, and samplers.

In the mid-twentieth century, a few women broke the sexual barriers to become successful visual artists. Georgia O'Keeffe painted the stark landscape of the Southwest. Lee Krasner and Grace Hartigan made their mark on the New York School of painting. Louise Nevelson created sculptures of greater and greater originality.

Creative women have gained recognition in a field that was overwhelmingly dominated by men until as recently as 1980. Myths about women's inability to sustain the creative urge have been slowly but surely eroded as women have fought to be accepted as equals in the world of the arts.

Above left: the sculptor Louise Nevelson in 1976. Above right: Georgia O'Keeffe, one of the pioneers of modern American art, with her painting Life and Death, *in 1931. Below: painter Margaret Neill in her studio.*

Chapter 7

In 1979 Judy Chicago exhibited The Dinner Party, *a work combining embroidery and ceramics and paying tribute to some of the great women down through the centuries.*

Some women painters today, rather than turning away from "women's work," look more closely at it, and through their canvases the viewer shares the intimacy of their homes. Barbara Rogers Soldwedel's paintings: Left, The Tyrant; *right,* Making Bread.

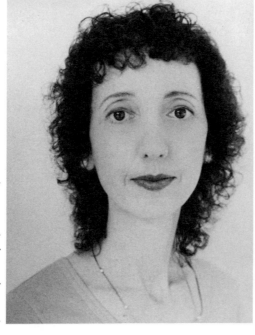

Left: Joyce Carol Oates, short story writer and novelist, who writes about contemporary America. Right: the poet and novelist Alice Walker, author of The Color Purple, *a wrenching story of growing up black, poor—and female.*

Is there a "women's art"? The answer is yes and no. Some women artists choose as their subject matter themes also used by male artists. Others choose to take as their theme "woman" and all that that word implies—"woman's work," "woman's role," "woman's psyche."

POETS, NOVELISTS, AND PLAYWRIGHTS

Not all heroes are armed with guns and swords. Many use their imaginations and pens to accomplish their ends, and among these are American women of talent and genius who turned to the writing of poetry. They used words as their "ammunition."

Phillis Wheatley, who rose from slavery, had her poetry published in 1773, when she was nineteen. Emily Dickinson received recognition only after her death in 1886. Her poems were called "the most readable, the most understandable and the most inspiring."

Edna St. Vincent Millay was a great lyric poet, whose sonnets have been compared favorably with romantic poets of the time of Shakespeare. In 1923, she was the first woman awarded the Pulitzer Prize for poetry. In 1960, poet Gwendolyn Brooks became the first black writer awarded the Pulitzer Prize.

Fiction writing has always been a favorite with women. Of the novels published before 1820 about one-third were written by women. Sarah Wentworth in 1781 was the author of the first novel written in America. Best remembered novels of the nineteenth century are Louisa May Alcott's book *Little Women* (1868), which made girlhood, its problems and its pleasures real for millions, and Harriet Beecher Stowe's *Uncle Tom's Cabin*, published in book form in 1852. America was shocked by Stowe's account of the cruelties and sorrows of slavery.

Edith Wharton in 1920 became the first woman to win the Pulitzer Prize for literature for her novel *The Age of Innocence*.

Pearl Buck wrote novels based on her experience as a missionary in China. *The Good Earth* established her as a world literary figure. In 1938 she became the first American woman to be awarded the Nobel Prize for literature.

Willa Cather was one of the great writers of short stories and novels of the twentieth century. Her stories dealt chiefly with her younger days.

Eudora Welty, Joyce Carol Oates, Toni Morrison, Joan Didion, and Anne Tyler are but a few of the prominent writers of today.

One of America's most forceful playwrights was Lillian Hellman, who was in the forefront of the fight for human rights in this century. *Watch on the Rhine* and *The Little Foxes* are but two of her contributions to the theater.

Amelia Earhart (1897-1937). In 1932 she became the first woman to fly alone across the Atlantic.

SCIENCE AND TECHNOLOGY

Joining with the men of science who occupied important positions were many women whose contributions were invaluable. They were qualified to become partners in the advanced research being conducted in such fields as space, computers, nuclear energy, and medicine. They have reached landmark achievements in problem-solving in the medical and biological sciences. They are prominently represented in the newer sciences, such as anthropology and psychology.

Margaret Mead (1901–1978). Anthropologist and writer, she emphasized the role of women in cultures of the world. Her books *Coming of Age in Samoa* and *Growing Up in New Guinea* are still widely read and debated today.

Rachel Carson (1907–1964). An ecologist, she contributed greatly toward developing American consciousness and concern for the environment through the publication of her book *Silent Spring* in 1962.

Barbara McClintock. In 1919, as a freshman at Cornell's College of Agriculture in Ithaca, New York, she hoped to major in plant breeding, but when she was told that women were not accepted in the department, she majored in botany instead. McClintock went on to perform brilliant research in the genetics of corn. For her work she received the Nobel Prize in 1983.

Rosalyn Yalow. Senior medical physicist, Yalow was the first American-trained woman to receive a Nobel Prize, which she was awarded in 1977 in Physiology or Medicine for the development of radio-immunoassay, a method that permits measurement of hormones and other substances in blood and body fluids.

Grace Hopper. The U.S. Navy's oldest officer on active duty until her retirement in 1986 at the age of 79, Rear Admiral Hopper was a leader in the computer revolution. She developed the computer language COBOL.

Marian Anderson achieved world fame as an opera and concert singer. Because she was black, she was denied the use of Constitution Hall in Washington, D.C., in 1932. Through the intercession of Eleanor Roosevelt, the U.S. government made the Lincoln Memorial available to her, where seventy-five thousand people heard her sing. In 1955 she became the first black woman to sing at the Metropolitan Opera. In the years since, she has been followed by other black divas such as Leontyne Price and Kathleen Battle.

THE PERFORMING ARTS

In the theater, movies, and nightclubs, on television and video cassettes, in opera and ballet, as performers, writers, producers, and directors, women have come into their own. This is another area of achievement that is no longer male-dominated. Who sets the pace for the young women and men today? The rock stars, the Tina Turners, the Cyndi Laupers, the Madonnas. Millions of records are sold, millions of dollars are made, millions of boys and girls, men and women, have become their faithful fans. The theater, for years completely male-dominated in writing, producing, and directing, has accepted women into the "sacred brotherhood," as have the motion picture and television studios.

Always visible in the past as renowned singers in front of the curtain in the world's great opera houses, women today are becoming the directors, conductors, and impresarios. Still to be achieved: greater representation in the best known orchestras where men continue to dominate.

Women first made their mark as performers on the stage. With the advent of the motion picture industry, new roles opened up for actresses, costume designers, and script writers. Today women are also in responsible positions as directors, producers, and studio executives.

Beverly Sills (right), after an outstanding singing career in opera, was appointed general director of the New York City Opera.

Sarah Caldwell (above), founder of the Opera Company of Boston, a composer and producer of operas, was the first woman to conduct at the Metropolitan Opera, in 1976—for a performance of *La Traviata* with Beverly Sills.

Jane Fonda, who has had a highly successful film career, is closely identified with the women's rights movement. She has written and made video cassettes on physical fitness for women, and she lectures widely on issues of concern to women.

Victoria Roche, the first girl ever to play in the Little League World Series, is shown here at Williamsport, Pennsylvania in August of 1984, as she leaves the field after her time at bat.

SPORTS

Equality in sports has traveled a long, hard road. It was traditionally believed that women were definitely "the weaker sex" and could therefore not qualify in sports that required great strength and stamina. Consider baseball, football, basketball, and other sports where girls and women were expected to be in the audience and not on the field. It was only under great pressure from feminists that girls were permitted to enroll in Little Leagues.

Changes followed the passage of Equality in Sports Programs legislation. In 1972, 7 percent of high school athletes were female; in 1984, 35 percent of high school athletes were female.

Whereas formerly the bulk of the money available for sports went into male sports and physical fitness programs, today female teams are provided with women coaches, equipment, and travel allowances.

In the 1970s and 1980s women champions were no longer the exception and no longer restricted to "feminine sports"; they became gymnasts, jockeys, and race-car drivers.

Today women by the millions are found in almost all sports on all levels, receiving greater financial support and recognition. Many barriers that have existed since ancient Greece (at that time only high priestesses were allowed even to watch Olympic sports events) are down.

A Study in Courage

Libby Riddles was the first woman to win the 1,135-mile (1,830-km) Alaskan dogsled race, in 1985. She "mushed" her thirteen-dog team across Alaska's ice fields and snowcapped mountains. It took her three weeks to make the grueling trek through blinding blizzards, across two mountain ranges and the Yukon River, from Anchorage to Nome, Alaska.

Billie Jean King (right, with glasses). First woman athlete ever to earn $100,000 in a year, in 1971.

Althea Gibson. First American black to win the singles title at Wimbledon in Britain, in 1957.

COMMUNICATIONS

It is true that more women are working in the news programs at the major networks than ever before.

There are women reporters and anchorpersons at almost every television station in the United States. According to one study, the increase in the number of women in the news is "a recent trend that parallels the movement into employment."

However, another study found that the growing numbers of women in communication don't reflect a substantial shift in power:

> The media elite—those leaders who influence Americans because of their position in the mass media—is composed mainly of white males in their thirties and forties.
>
> One in twenty is nonwhite.
>
> One in five is female.
>
> One in twelve is following "in his father's footsteps as a second generation journalist."

Katherine Graham has been called "the most powerful woman in America." Taking over the leadership of the Washington Post Company when her husband died in 1963, she not only increased sales but made the newspaper a leader in investigative reporting.

Charlayne Hunter-Gault is the New York-based correspondent for the MacNeil/Lehrer NewsHour. *She has won numerous awards for excellence in journalism, including two National News and Documentary Emmy Awards. Hunter-Gault was the first black woman to attend the University of Georgia.*

Top Ranking Women in the Media

PBS: Judy Woodruff and Charlayne Hunter-Gault.

CBS: Diane Sawyer and Lesley Stahl.

NBC: Jane Pauley and Connie Chung.

ABC: Barbara Walters and Kathleen Sullivan.

Newsweek magazine and the *Washington Post*: Katharine Graham, chief executive.

Syndicated columnists: Erma Bombeck, Ellen Goodman, and Ann Landers.

CHAPTER 8

WOMEN TODAY

The position of women has changed dramatically, as you have read. Barriers still exist but are being reduced. Many of these changes have been brought about through more favorable legislation—changes in political, economic, and social conditions; in marriage, divorce, family relationships and life-styles, family roles and size; and among minority women and older women.

Yet there are still powerful forces that make it virtually impossible to take advantage of new opportunities that *appear* to be available to women. Women's worth and contributions are not fully recognized by law. And although stereotypes, misimpressions, and fears are being reduced, they still exist.

The goal of equal rights is far from being won, but there have been great changes. Let us look at some of them.

THE FAMILY

The structure of the family has had both dramatic change and acceptance. We can no longer consider that it consists of mother, father, and offspring. Both women and men find themselves in the process of redesigning their lives as single parents or working parents. Children often come home to an empty house. These "latch-key children" are no longer few in number, and their problems are many. The 1970s and 1980s can be described as the decades during which this situation became chronic. These years saw more than half of all women, sixteen years and over, working outside the home—either by choice or because of a need to contribute funds to the upkeep of the home.

Role changes became extremely common, as men recog-

72

Coming home to the family after a hard day's work at the office

nized the need to assume household duties. They proved themselves capable of cooking, doing the laundry, cleaning, and caring for children. Some actually admit that they enjoy the change. It used to be said that "women's work is never done." True! But now it is beginning to be shared by men, and there is no longer a stigma attached to it. One-parent families are on the increase. Most have fared well, despite the fact that two parents *are* better than one, in most cases.

The sharing of household responsibilities and the trend toward smaller families have made it possible for women to consider many new options available when their childbearing years are over. When housing facilities and child-care centers are more available, women will be able to fill more and more important positions outside the home.

THE QUEST
FOR EQUALITY

Women have fought hard in their battle for equality with men. The strong push for equal opportunity for women took place on local, state, and national levels. Women used the following procedures in their quest:

They used the courts for litigation.

They set up public meetings to educate the public.

They lobbied legislators and candidates.

They secured editorial and civic leader support.

They organized at the national, state, and local level.

The following federal laws that protect women were the result:

Social Security Act (1935) and amendments provide for monthly retirement and disability to male and female workers and for survivors' benefits to dependents of workers—male and female—covered by the system.

Unemployment insurance is managed jointly by the federal and state governments. Benefits are paid for loss of job through no fault of either male or female employee. Benefits vary from state to state. This is part of the social security system that began making payments in 1938.

Fair Labor Standards Act (1938) guarantees minimum wage and overtime pay for men and women employed in businesses that fall under federal regulation.

Equal Pay Act of 1963 was the first federal law against sex discrimination in employment. It prohibits employers from discriminating between employees on the basis of sex by paying different wages for equal work requiring equal skills, effort, and responsibility, and performed under similar working conditions.

Words that Need Defining

Feminism

The word *feminism* represents a broad concept that needs to be examined carefully. In simple terms, it merely means that women *can* be the equal of men. It does not carry with it the idea of militancy but rather the desire for change. That change must be embodied in the laws governing the political, social, and economic status of women. The movement to accomplish these changes became popular in the 1970s. We still hear names that were given to this push for equality: women's liberation (or "women's lib" for short), women's movement, feminist movement, women's rights movement.

What gave rise to this feminist movement was the change in the lives of women themselves. They entered the labor force in large numbers. Their family size began to decrease and their life expectancy increased. Women began to choose nontraditional roles. Many remained single by choice. Many others became single through divorce or widowhood. No longer was the image of women that of wife and mother exclusively.

Gender Gap

Another common phrase that needs to be defined is *gender gap*. Simply expressed, it means the separation, inequality, and disparity between men and women, and it also means another thing—those inequalities in income, jobs, politics, and roles in state and national government. It extends to social acceptance. It means restrictions in such fields as religion and education, in sports and recreation, even in admissions into clubs and once exclusively male organizations.

Women had become locked into traditional jobs. They were expected to apply only for such jobs as secretarial, sales, service, clerical, and factory. An income gap accompanied this gender gap. It was attributed to differences in education and work experience.

One Woman Who Broke the Gender Gap

Geraldine Ferraro, a member of the House of Representatives, was nominated in 1984 as vice-presidential candidate by the Democratic party. Never before had a major party nominated a woman as a member of the presidential ticket. In accepting the nomination by acclamation, Ferraro stated, "America is a land where dreams come true for all citizens. . . . There are no doors we cannot unlock. We will place no limit on achievement. If we can do this, we can do anything."

Chapter 8

Contemporary Leaders of the Women's Movement

Betty Friedan (right) wrote *The Feminine Mystique* in 1963. The book signaled the rebirth of feminism. It led many women to question their place in American society and to join organizations to seek change. She launched the contemporary women's movement by depicting "the home as a domestic penal institution for women" (i.e., prison). She was the first leader of the National Organization of Women (NOW).

Gloria Steinem (left) was the founder and editor of *Ms.* magazine in 1971. She advocated equal pay for equal work, child-care centers, the right to abortion, and the election of women to political office.

Susan Brownmiller (right) wrote *Against Our Will*, about rape of women, and promoted women's rights.

Kate Millet (left), the author of
Sexual Politics, described the
"power struggle between the
sexes."

Eleanor Smeal (right), president
of NOW, speaking at Smith
College in 1983: "Women
were not born Republicans,
Democrats, or yesterday."

Aileen Hernandez (left) was
president of NOW in 1970 and
served for eighteen months
(1965–1966) as the only
woman member of the Equal
Employment Opportunities
Commission.

77

One out of four children is now being raised by a single parent, usually the mother. The number of households headed by women with no husband present doubled between 1970 and 1985 and has tripled since 1960.

One-third of all households headed by women are "poor." Two of three adults in poverty are women.

Seventy percent of single parents work outside the home. In more than one-half of two-parent families, both parents work.

Title VII of the Civil Rights Act of 1964 makes it unlawful for any employer to "fail or refuse to hire or discharge any individual or otherwise to discriminate against any individual with respect to compensation, terms or conditions or privileges of employment because of such individual's race, color, religion, sex, or national origin." (An amendment in 1978 prohibited discrimination in employment because of pregnancy.) Title VII is administered by the Equal Employment Opportunity Commission (EEOC), which prohibited "help wanted—male" and "help wanted—female" advertisements.

Occupational Safety and Health Act (OSHA) of 1970 assures safe and healthful working conditions for employees.

Equal Employment Opportunity Act (EEOA) of 1970 strengthened the powers of the EEOC to bring suits in court after an investigation. It includes widened coverage of the Civil Rights Act to embrace employers and unions of eight or more workers, employees of state and federal government, and employees of educational institutions. It protects employees against sexual harassment, such as unwelcome sexual advances, requests for sexual favors, and other verbal or physical conduct of a sexual nature.

Title IX Educational Act (amendments) of 1972 prohibits sex discrimination in any elementary, secondary, or post-secondary school if the institution receives any federal monies. The implementation of this law has become a battleground between liberals and conservatives.

Retirement Equity Act (1984), known as the "women's bill," provides a wife with retirement benefits after her husband's death. It also gives a wife limited pension benefits should the husband die before reaching retirement age.

Affirmative action seeks to overcome discrimination and the exclusion of women and minorities from hiring and promotion in

Above left: a bond trader on Wall Street. Under the Equal Pay Act of 1963, employers are prohibited from paying women less than is paid to men for the same type of work. Above right: women have gained the right to remain in the work force through their pregnancies. Expectant mother Karin Gustavsson-Jackson on the job.

Left: women at work in the Postal Service. The Civil Rights Act of 1964 prohibits racial discrimination.

public and private employment and from enrollment in colleges and professional schools. In some cases, quotas and preferential treatment were given to women, blacks, and Hispanics. Federal laws and policies encourage the use of sex and race quotas as remedial devices in allocating jobs and educational opportunities. Many court cases have followed, dealing with hiring, promotion, wage policies, and seniority rights (during job layoffs, seniority principles have a devastating effect on the recently hired women and minorities). Affirmative action is looked upon as a temporary policy until women and minorities gain a foothold in the economy.

OTHER FORMS OF DISCRIMINATION REDUCED

Membership in all-male clubs was significantly reduced by the Supreme Court decision that forbade the exclusion of women from such organizations as Rotary and the Junior Chamber of Commerce.

In the 1970s and 1980s many forms of pregnancy discrimination—including forced leave, loss of seniority, lack of medical coverage, and outright dismissal—were challenged, primarily in the courts. Under the Pregnancy Discrimination Act of 1978, women who decide to leave their jobs because of pregnancy lose nothing and may get payment for medical and hospital expenses.

The law does *not* require women to remain on the job. Employers may not penalize women who become pregnant or who have a child. It outlaws the loss of seniority by women when they return to work after childbirth.

ABORTION

In 1973, the United States Supreme Court ruled in a landmark decision that it was unconstitutional for states to prohibit abortions since it was a private decision between doctor and patient. It liberalized the availability of abortion to women (*Doe* v. *Bolton*; *Roe* v. *Wade*). Many states repealed their legislation that prohibited abortion. The "Right to Life" groups have built up much pressure to add a constitutional amendment to bar abortions.

STATE LABOR LAWS

All of the fifty states, the District of Columbia, and Puerto Rico have laws affecting some aspect of women's employment—workmen's compensation, minimum wages and hours, and harsh working conditions. New state laws provide many women with protection against substandard wages and hours as were first provided by the Fair Labor Standards Act of 1938.

Some states have specified in their constitutions that equal rights or equal protection may not be denied because of sex.

CHAPTER 9

THE STRUGGLE CONTINUES

Changes do not come about overnight. On the surface it may seem that the status of American women is vastly superior to that of women in many other nations. But remember, that is on the surface. Look deeper into the so-called changes. What we find is that there is still considerable discrimination. Society still feels that there is "man's work" and "woman's work." From early childhood we find that there are differences in the toys available for boys versus girls. It is found that girls are not encouraged to go much further than elementary mathematics. Unless they make an effort, they are not encouraged to take advanced science courses. Mechanics, electronics, industrial and technical trades are not presented to girls as desirable alternatives to cooking and clerical courses. What this has done is to reinforce the concept that the role of women in society should re-

main a passive one. Not fair? Of course not. Not tolerable? It has not been. Women no longer accept any rockbound conclusions as to where they can go and what they can achieve. The future is *now*.

EMPLOYMENT

Experts admit that American women still face job discrimination that is deep and pervasive. It will be many years before parity with male workers is achieved. Among the factors that still limit women's progress in employment are low-paying jobs, household responsibilities, lack of job security and seniority, scarcity of child-care facilities, and fewer choices of employment. Occupational segregation continues despite laws that were intended to eliminate sex bias. One-fourth of all employed women accounted for segregation into just twenty-two of the five hundred occupations enumerated by the U.S. Census. The figures in the chart on page 85 indicate occupations in which women predominate—"women's work." Some of the highest-paying and prestigious occupations—those with less than 30 percent women—are traditionally "men's work."

Discrimination and lack of preparation explain the relatively poor economic position of women. Yet determined and able women are slowly moving into jobs traditionally reserved for men. The proof of this is that from 1970 to 1980 women became more numerous in such jobs as accounting, banking, and janitorial work. They also entered into such formerly male occupations as pharmacist, public relations specialist, insurance adjustor, and even bartender.

Research has also shown that as more and more women entered the job market, the salary scale seems to have fallen. A majority of emerging jobs seem to be in heavily segregated and exclusively female occupations. The projections for the 1990s seem to indicate that very little will change in either segregation or occupations available. More work lies ahead for those who advocate change and improvement.

MINORITIES

In the United States there is no official list of minorities as such.

However, the government has identified several groups as being in need of special attention. This grouping lists the following: women, blacks, Hispanics, Asians, Pacific Islanders, American Indians, and Eskimos. Why women? They are not a racial group, nor are they an ethnic group. As a majority of the population in the United States, women face many of the same obstacles as do minority group males.

In addition, many new jobs that are being filled by women in banking, insurance, and high-tech industries are found in suburban areas which are not accessible to black, Hispanic, and Asian women.

Also legislation that created "equal employment opportunities" and "affirmative action" has not been effective. Minorities continue to find discrimination in jobs, wages, and promotion. Unemployment among minority women has since the 1950s been 78 percent higher than that of white women.

A LESSER LIFE

Did you know that in more than one hundred countries new mothers receive paid, job-protected time off? The United States is not one of those countries. In 1986 Sylvia Ann Hewlett published *A Lesser Life: The Myth of Women's Liberation in America*. To the dismay of many she pointed out that American women, in spite of their

Left: lawyers Janet Benshoof and Isabelle Katz Pinzler of the American Civil Liberties Union (ACLU) are in the forefront of the women's rights movement. According to Pinzler, "the major goals of the women's rights movement have not yet been achieved." Below left: of protective service workers (i.e., police, fire fighters, etc.), 13.2 percent are women. Below right: of registered nurses, 95.1 percent are women.

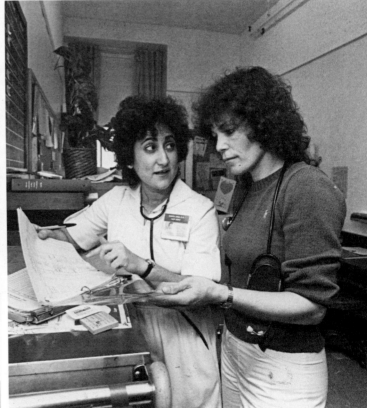

Above left: of elementary teachers, 84 percent are women. Above right: of airline pilots and navigators, 2.6 percent are women. Right: of telephone operators, 88.8 percent are women.

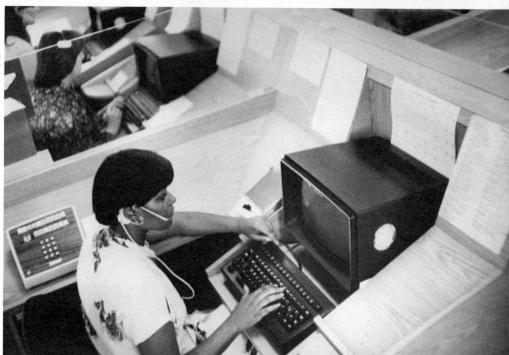

Women as a Percentage of All Persons Employed in Selected Occupations

Occupation	Percent Women
Librarians	87.
Registered Nurses	95.1
Teachers (except College and University)	73.
Elementary School Teachers	84.
Bank Tellers	93.
Bookkeepers, Accounting and Auditing Clerks	91.5
Cashiers	83.1
Receptionists	97.6
Secretaries	98.4
Telephone Operators	88.8
Engineers	6.7
Lawyers and Judges	18.2
Physicians, Dentists and related practitioners	14.8
Airline Pilots and Navigators	2.6
Executive, Administrative, and Managerial	35.6
Mechanics and Repairers	3.1
Protective Service Workers (Police, Fire Fighters, etc.)	13.2

Source: United States Department of Labor, Bureau of Labor Statistics, January 1986.

Chapter 9   **Sexism Exists in Language**

Many reflections of sexist thinking exist in our language. For example: "All men are created equal."

Some suggestions:

Men and women should be referred to as people and not primarily as members of the opposite sex.

Gender differences should not be highlighted, but men and women's shared humanity and common attributes should be stressed.

Members of both sexes should be represented as whole human beings with human strengths and weaknesses and not masculine or feminine ones.

Men and women should be treated equally with respect, dignity, and seriousness.

Occupational terms ending in *man* should be replaced wherever possible by terms that include members of either sex, unless they refer to a particular person.

---

achievements in education and the workplace, are far behind their European sisters economically, that American working women—often single parents—have had to become "super-women" as breadwinners and homemakers. "Not only is the wage gap—the gap between what men and women earn—the same as it was fifty years ago, but there are real shockers out there, like 25 percent of all women working full time earn less than $10,000 a year." Among Hewlett's recommendations is a greater emphasis on the importance of childbirth:

prenatal care and medical coverage for childbirth.

FEMALE HARASSMENT AT THE WORKPLACE

In 1986 the U.S. Supreme Court ruled unanimously that employers may be sued for sexual harassment on the job. The judges ruled that unwelcome sexual advances, as well as other misconduct that creates a "hostile environment" for workers, are sufficient to sustain claims of illegal sex discrimination.

CHAPTER 10

LOOKING TO THE TWENTY-FIRST CENTURY

Women, young and old and those in between, can look toward the twenty-first century with confidence and anticipation. There will be choices that were only dreamed of in the past, and doors have been opened that once seemed forever closed.

WOMEN IN THE LABOR FORCE

Projections indicate that there will be more women in the labor force by the year 2000 than ever before in history. Fewer and fewer couples will live in the traditional relationships that found men working outside the home in support of a stay-at-home wife and family. Jobs, careers, raising a family, and taking care of a home will be influenced in the future.

THE FUTURE OF WOMEN IN POLITICS

One of the major objectives of the women's movement is to elect more women to office to assure that progress toward equality will continue. Few women today can be classified as "power brokers"—women with "clout," women with power to make national and international decisions. Women will strive for positions in which they can influence public policy: elected offices, judiciary posts, union positions, appointive jobs in government.

WOMEN'S CHANGING ROLE IN THE FAMILY

In the 1980s there was evidence that the attitudes toward marriage

*A doctor at the New York Hospital-Cornell
Medical Center in New York City*

A Look Ahead for Women

In 1985 more than 40 percent of all women were in the work force.

Projection for 1990:   Forty-five percent of women of all ages are expected to be in the work force.

Projection for 1980s and 1990s: Women are expected to take seven out of ten new jobs that are created.

By the year 2000:   Women's wages will be 74 percent of men's wages. Women will be moving into higher-paying occupations.

*A mother enrolled in the University of Michigan's
Center for Continuing Education of Women is shown
here using the card catalog in the library.*

Accountants will be in demand in the twenty-first-century business world.

Older women who are retiring today receive better retirement benefits and are more likely to have supplemental pensions and other assets, compared to working women in previous generations.

Where the Jobs Will Be

High demand is predicted for women in the following fields:

Technical occupations   Statisticians, computer technicians, surveyors, projectionists, solar energy technicians, machinists, broadcast technicians

Mechanics and repairers   Appliance maintenance and repair, locksmiths, railway mechanics, computer maintenance and repair

Industrial production   Printing, foundry work

Service occupations   Protective and custodial services

Sales   Appliance sales, auto services, auto parts counter work

Transportation   Air, merchant marines, trucking, railroads

Law enforcement   Public and private protective services

Agriculture, forestry, fisheries   Soil conservationists, forestry technicians, fish farmers, landscape and nursery workers

Engineering and science   Technicians and mechanics of all kinds

Business   Accountants, insurance agents, sales personnel for wholesale manufacturing and appliances

Legal assistants

Physical therapy

Some women may lose employment because of automation and the impact of computers on office work. On the other hand, affirmative action will increase job openings.

and family were changing. The traditional marriage, in which the husband is the sole breadwinner and the wife stays home with the children is becoming the exception, not the rule. Women are waiting until much later—age thirty-five to forty—to start families as compared with the nineteen- and twenty-year-olds of years ago. In addition, the divorce rate has increased, and there were more single parents.

INCOME PROSPECTS FOR THE FUTURE

"Comparable pay—comparable worth" is likely to be a controversial labor issue in the 1980s and 1990s. Advocates urge that men and women be paid the same amount for jobs of "comparable worth." The concept of comparable worth suggests that equal wages be paid for jobs considered of equal value to an employer.

Chapter 10

A student from the older generation returning to school to complete her education

More women are found to be working alongside men in occupations requiring higher skills.

Jobs would be measured in terms of skill, effort, training, education, responsibility, and working conditions.

One of the major difficulties with the "comparable worth" idea is that no objective standards have as yet been established. Supporters of comparable worth state that women are systematically and illegally paid less for doing work that may be different yet just as difficult as that done by men. For example:

Wall washers earn more than practical nurses.

Garbage collectors earn more than teachers.

Electricians are predominantly male and make twice as much as secretaries, 99 percent of whom are women.

Opponents of comparable pay for comparable worth state: Pay should be determined on the principle of "equal pay for equal work."

The marketplace should determine the value of a job.

There is no objective way to measure a job's worth.

The debate on comparable pay for comparable worth is on! An answer is needed to "What are 'equal work' and 'equal value' "?

WOMEN IN THE YEAR 2000

The dramatic changes of the 1960s, 1970s, and 1980s pose new and awesome questions for today's women. The average American woman has more than thirty years of activity available to her after her youngest child enters school. Never before have women had such a broad range of choices open to them as to how they will spend their lives. Careers, independence, and single life have been made enticingly attractive and at times lonely and even dangerous. So many choices are facing women that a growing problem of priorities confronts them. More and more women have elected to forgo marriage or to marry later in life, or to marry and forgo having children for the sake of independence or a career. Expanded educational opportunities, including new community colleges and adult education programs at all levels, have opened and will continue to provide new choices for women. American women have been confronted by great challenges before. Can tomorrow's women adapt to changes being brought about by the social, political, and economic forces shaping the United States today? And will they be in the vanguard of those who work to bring about change? We think they will.

INDEX

94

Index